DyslexiaGames.co

Puzzling Patterns
Puzzles & Patterns Games to Challenge the Mind

30 GAMES

Games to Train the Mind to Correct Reading Problems Associated with Dyslexia and Symbol Confusion.

The Thinking Tree

Copyright © 2011 the Thinking Tree, LLC
All rights reserved.

Dyslexia Games Series A, Book 2
Friendly Copyright Notice:

ALL DYSLEXIA GAMES, WORKSHEETS, AND MATERIALS MAY <u>NOT</u> BE SHARED, COPIED, EMAILED, OR OTHERWISE DISTRIBUTED TO ANYONE OUTSIDE YOUR HOUSEHOLD OR IMMEDIATE FAMILY (SHARING IS STEALING).

Please refer people interested in Dyslexia Games to our website to purchase their own copy of the materials.

The Thinking Tree LLC • 617 N Swope St. • Greenfield, IN 46140 • info@dyslexiagames.com • (317) 622-8852

Puzzling Patterns
Puzzles & Patterns Games to Challenge the Mind

By Sarah J. Brown

Parent Teacher Instructions:

Provide the student with a set of colored markers and a fine point black pen.

This workbook taps into the child's creativity and natural problem solving skills. The goal is to figure out what is missing and draw it. As the lessons progress, they become more challenging.

These exercises develop tracking skills, memory skills, problem solving skills, teach symbol recognition, and the importance of left, right, up and down.

Allow the child to use 2 to 4 worksheets per day. These exercises are fun but can be overstimulating for the mind if the child is expected to complete several pages at once. So, start with two or three, and if the child asks for more give him another, but then encourage him to wait for tomorrow. It's good to stop before the child becomes overstimulated by the puzzles.

Name:_____ Date:_____

www.DyslexiaGames.com   "Finally, a fun solution for reading confusion!"

© 2011 all rights reserved. The Thinking Tree, LLC

Name:_____ **Date:**_____

www.DyslexiaGames.com   "Finally, a fun solution for reading confusion!"

© 2011 all rights reserved. The Thinking Tree, LLC

dice and dots

Name:_____ Date:_____

www.DyslexiaGames.com   "Finally, a fun solution for reading confusion!"

© 2011 all rights reserved. The Thinking Tree, LLC

dice and dots

Name:_____ Date:_____

www.DyslexiaGames.com   "Finally, a fun solution for reading confusion!"

© 2011 all rights reserved. The Thinking Tree, LLC

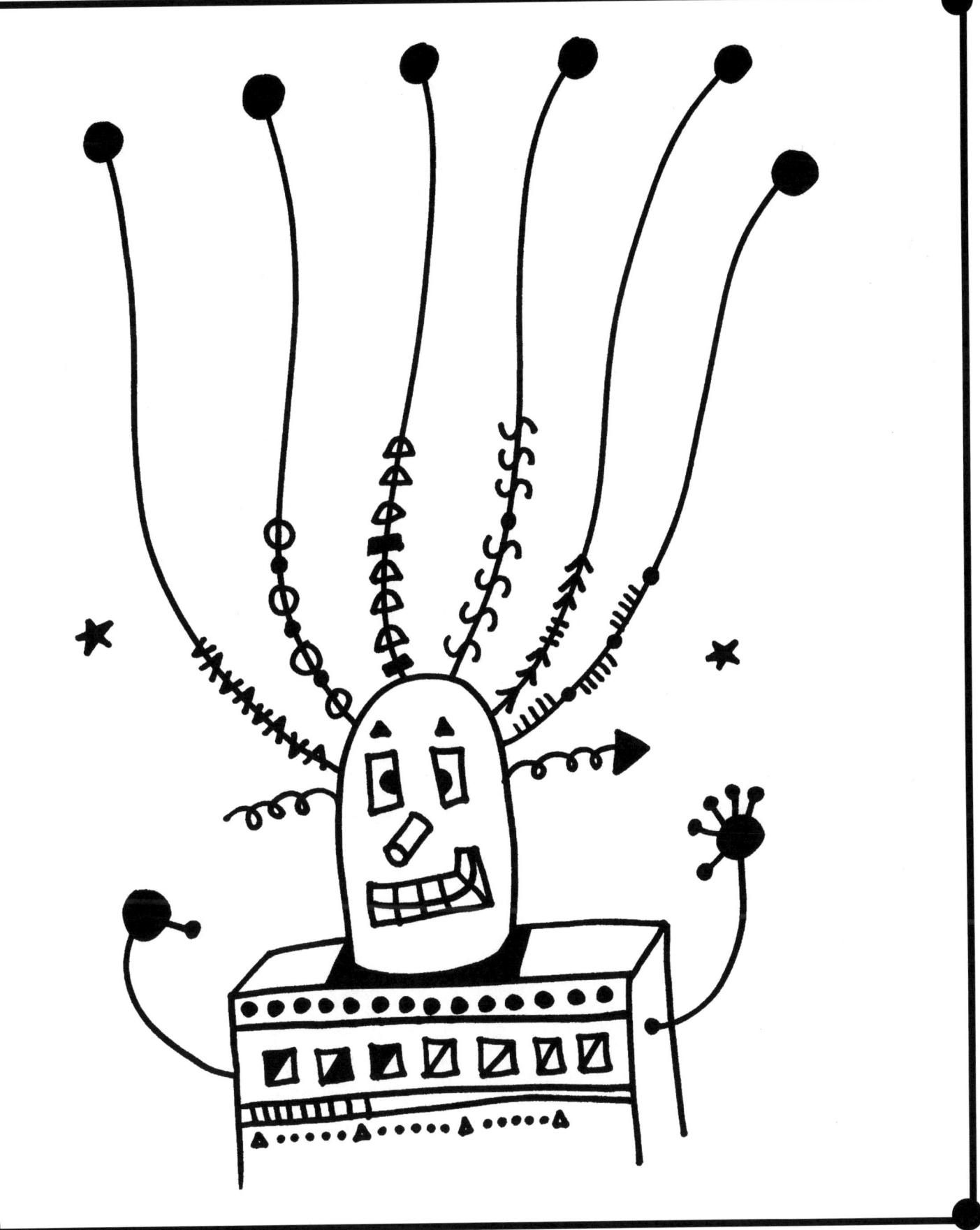

Name:_____ **Date:**_____

www.DyslexiaGames.com   "Finally, a fun solution for reading confusion!"

© 2011 all rights reserved. The Thinking Tree, LLC

Name:_____ **Date:**_____

www.DyslexiaGames.com   "Finally, a fun solution for reading confusion!"

© 2011 all rights reserved. The Thinking Tree, LLC

Name:_____ Date:_____

www.DyslexiaGames.com   "Finally, a fun solution for reading confusion!"

© 2011 all rights reserved. The Thinking Tree, LLC

dice and dots

Name:_____ Date:_____

www.DyslexiaGames.com   "Finally, a fun solution for reading confusion!"

© 2011 all rights reserved. The Thinking Tree, LLC

Name:_____ Date:_____

www.DyslexiaGames.com   "Finally, a fun solution for reading confusion!"

© 2011 all rights reserved. The Thinking Tree, LLC

Name:_____ Date:_____

www.DyslexiaGames.com   "Finally, a fun solution for reading confusion!"

© 2011 all rights reserved. The Thinking Tree, LLC

Name:_____ **Date:**_____

www.DyslexiaGames.com   "Finally, a fun solution for reading confusion!"

© 2011 all rights reserved. The Thinking Tree, LLC

Name _____ DyslexiaGames.com "Finally, a fun solution Date _____ ding confusion!"

© 2011 all rights reserved. The Thinking Tree, LLC

Name:_____ Date:_____

www.DyslexiaGames.com   "Finally, a fun solution for reading confusion!"

© 2011 all rights reserved. The Thinking Tree, LLC

os·tos·tos·t

>ē>·>ē>·>ē

Φm·Φm·Φm·

a··a··a··a··a··

Name:_____ Date:_____

www.DyslexiaGames.com   "Finally, a fun solution for reading confusion!"

© 2011 all rights reserved. The Thinking Tree, LLC

Name:_____ Date:_____

www.DyslexiaGames.com   "Finally, a fun solution for reading confusion!"

© 2011 all rights reserved. The Thinking Tree, LLC

Name:_____ Date:_____

www.DyslexiaGames.com "Finally, a fun solution for reading confusion!"

© 2011 all rights reserved. The Thinking Tree, LLC

Name:_____ Date:_____

www.DyslexiaGames.com "Finally, a fun solution for reading confusion!"

© 2011 all rights reserved. The Thinking Tree, LLC

Name:_____ Date:_____

www.DyslexiaGames.com   "Finally, a fun solution for reading confusion!"

© 2011 all rights reserved. The Thinking Tree, LLC

★ ■ ⊙ _ _ _ _   > ■ 🍬 🍬 ∅
_ _ _ _ _ _ _ _
🍬
_ _ _ _ _   ♥ ✗ ∽ 🍬 ■

♥ = w   🍬 = m   ✗ = o
★ = f   ↑ = y   > = g
■ = u   ♦ = z   ↓ = p
▲ = ?   ⊙ = n   ∽ = r
⊃ = x   ∅ = y   ■ = s

Name:_____ Date:_____

www.DyslexiaGames.com   "Finally, a fun solution for reading confusion!"

© 2011 all rights reserved. The Thinking Tree, LLC

Name:_____ Date:_____

www.DyslexiaGames.com   "Finally, a fun solution for reading confusion!"

© 2011 all rights reserved. The Thinking Tree, LLC

copy cats

d b p q d b p q

b p d b d

d b q d b p q

b p q d p

d p d b q

Name:_____ Date:_____

www.DyslexiaGames.com   "Finally, a fun solution for reading confusion!"

© 2011 all rights reserved. The Thinking Tree, LLC

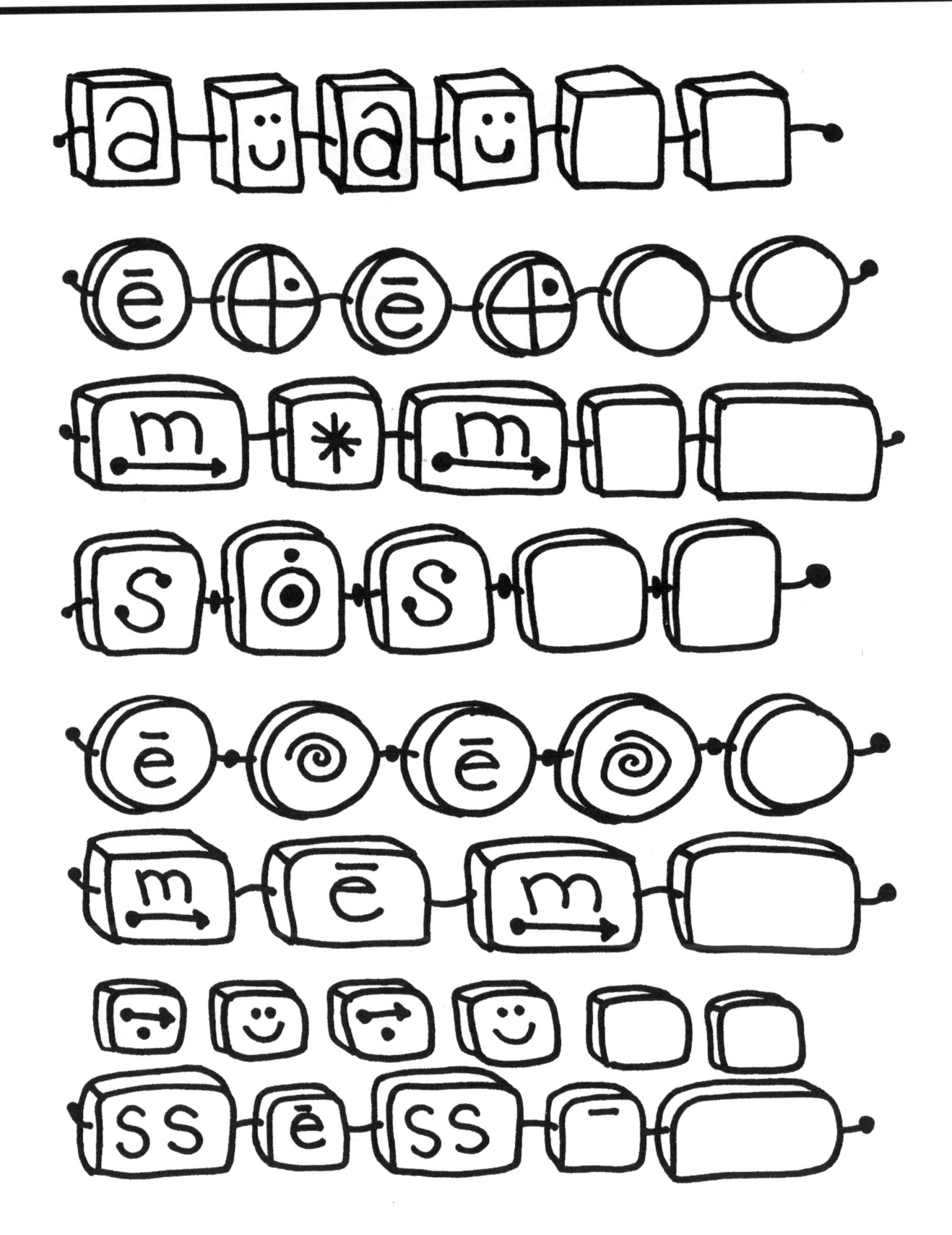

Name:_____ Date:_____

www.DyslexiaGames.com   "Finally, a fun solution for reading confusion!"

© 2011 all rights reserved. The Thinking Tree, LLC

Name: _____ Date: _____

www.DyslexiaGames.com   "Finally, a fun solution for reading confusion!"

© 2011 all rights reserved. The Thinking Tree, LLC

Name:_____ Date:_____

www.DyslexiaGames.com   "Finally, a fun solution for reading confusion!"

© 2011 all rights reserved. The Thinking Tree, LLC

Name:_____ Date:_____

www.DyslexiaGames.com   "Finally, a fun solution for reading confusion!"

© 2011 all rights reserved. The Thinking Tree, LLC

v d v d

b e b e

a 3 a 3

Name:_____ Date:_____

www.DyslexiaGames.com   "Finally, a fun solution for reading confusion!"

© 2011 all rights reserved. The Thinking Tree, LLC

Puzzling Patterns

Certificate of Completion

_____

Name & Age

_____

Date of Completion

The Thinking
TREE

Dyslexia Games

_____

Teacher

The Thinking TREE

www.DyslexiaGames.com

Copyright © 2011 the Thinking Tree, LLC
All rights reserved.

Created by: Sarah Janisse Brown

Puzzling Patterns

DyslexiaGames.com

Art Games, Puzzles & Patterns

30 GAMES

"Finally, a fun solution for reading confusion!"

DyslexiaGames.com

Dyslexia Games Series A
- ART FIRST — 30 GAMES
- Puzzling Patterns — 30 GAMES
- Letter Writing Games — 30 GAMES
- Draw & Spell — 30 GAMES
- Practice Pages — 30 Worksheets
- Word Hunt 1 — 30 Fun Games

Dyslexia Games Series B
- BRAIN FOOD — 30 Fun Lessons
- I.Q. Challenge — 30 GAMES
- Practice Pages 2 — 30 Worksheets
- Animal Art — 30 Fun Lessons
- Animal Talk — 30 Fun Lessons
- Word Hunt 2 — 30 Fun Games
- Creative Copywork — 45 Fun Lessons
- Silly Animal Rhymes — 30 RHYMES

Made in the USA
Columbia, SC
13 December 2024